WHERE SHALL I WANDER

WHERE SHALL I WANDER

new poems

John Ashbery

John Ashbery (signature)

ecco

An Imprint of HarperCollinsPublishers

HarperCollins books may be purchased for educational, business, or sales
promotional use. For information please write: Special Markets Department,
HarperCollins Publishers Inc., 10 East 53rd Street, New York, NY 10022.

FIRST EDITION

Designed by Mary Austin Speaker

Library of Congress Cataloging-in-Publication Data

Ashbery, John.
Where shall I wander : new poems / John Ashbery. — 1st ed.
p. cm.
ISBN 0-06-076529-1
I. Title.

PS3501.S475W47 2005
811'.54—dc22   2004053267

05 06 07 08 09 ❖/RRD 10 9 8 7 6 5 4 3 2 1

for David

ACKNOWLEDGMENTS

———

The author gratefully acknowledges the following publications in which poems in *Where Shall I Wander* first appeared, sometimes in slightly different form: *The American Poetry Review, Annals of Scholarship, Conjunctions, Denver Quarterly, Jubilat, The London Review of Books, The New York Review of Books, The New Yorker, The Paris Review, PN Review, Poetry Review* (UK), *The Poker, Shiny, The Times Literary Supplement,* and *Verse.*

CONTENTS

WHERE SHALL I WANDER

IGNORANCE OF THE LAW IS NO EXCUSE

We were warned about spiders, and the occasional famine.
We drove downtown to see our neighbors. None of them were home.
We nestled in yards the municipality had created,
reminisced about other, different places—
but were they? Hadn't we known it all before?

In vineyards where the bee's hymn drowns the monotony,
we slept for peace, joining in the great run.
He came up to me.
It was all as it had been,
except for the weight of the present,
that scuttled the pact we made with heaven.
In truth there was no cause for rejoicing,
nor need to turn around, either.
We were lost just by standing,
listening to the hum of wires overhead.

We mourned that meritocracy which, wildly vibrant,
had kept food on the table and milk in the glass.
In skid-row, slapdash style
we walked back to the original rock crystal he had become,
all concern, all fears for us.
We went down gently
to the bottom-most step. There you can grieve and breathe,
rinse your possessions in the chilly spring.
Only beware the bears and wolves that frequent it
and the shadow that comes when you expect dawn.

O FORTUNA

Good luck! Best wishes! The best of luck!
The very best! Godspeed! God bless you!
Peace be with you!
May your shadow never be less!
We can see through to the other side,
you see. It's your problem, we know,
but I can't help feeling a little envious.
What if darkness became unhinged right now?
Boomingly, swimmingly one remounts the current.
Here is where the shade was, the suggestion of flowers,
and peace, in another place.

Our competition is like tools of a certain order.
No one would have found them useful at first.
It wasn't until a real emergency arose, that someone
had the sense to recognize for what it was.
All hell didn't break loose, it was like a rising psalm
materializing like snow on an unseen mountain.
All that was underfoot was good, but lost.

AFFORDABLE VARIETY

It is one thing for a child to kidnap a parent.
It is quite another for the parent to sit down with the child,
blocking the path and its favorite mosses.

Cathexis arrives early in a golden coach.
We see stuff perched around,
mazes stuck in mazes,
knot of grapes at the throat, the horizon.

And we couldn't keep it coming.
That is so.

This is an invaded country.
Dawn will abdicate all your book.

Walking around will tell the important things:
discount ways, barrels of breakers,
days swept into being.

The child grew up as these things grew,
listened and was worried for the starched moments
dropped from the official record. We bought pants
and suits, the occasional gray shirt.
By week's end all was silence and industry.

DAYS OF RECKONING

Questions about the timing
intruded. The last client
before dawn was seen at a certain
distance. Then they brought up

the whole other issue of belonging.
Seems we weren't welcome despite
having occupied Hollyhock House
for generations upon generations.

Then a more remote client raised "issues"
closer to one, like a warm breeze from the cape,
seen to oscillate in an argument—
vexed particles. The captain was really sad

about that one. He came selling articles
door to door, from time to time. A personage
much beloved and little thought of.
He'd bought his first perimeter

with a baby tooth at the age of six.
Afterwards, when they asked him how he felt
about it, he was evasive, but in a way
that charmed every hearer. Dogs knew him

as a faithful friend, and tinkers
always had a stray dam for him.
Growing up lively in the house,
his ears soon pierced its roof.

At sixteen he attended his first dance,
met the charming Miss Letty.
There was another claimant, elusive,
predatory, veering to elvish embroilment

when the territories were divvied up at last.
The maid sent to say they could come down
if a clean breast were to be made of it.
As happened, that very evening, as I and others

can attest. The captain looked spiffy in his garb.
Rubies lurked in beads of lamplight, the joint
was carved and tears washed down with wine
whose bitter taste endures to this day.

WASTREL

Dear spit, the week is turning over
with the world. All is angry shouting outdoors.
I feel like one of St. Ursula's virgins
taking a last look at shelving rock and tree,
sailing into what must be the ineffable
if indeed it means anything to itself.

Tomorrow the stone judge will be here,
then more and more pioneers,
covering the basin as far as one can see
into blue beginnings. They have their place
in the populations, but are nominally
no more than we, planted here to survey them
and moving backward with sips of the tide.

We knew the tower bridge was jury-rigged,
the spirit spoof a trickle in the eye of God
we behold from a questioning though necessary
distance. In summer it was straw hats and licorice,
which, fading, leave a taste for other novelties
and sundries. It is never too late for stealth,
mourning itself, or the other irregular phantoms.

COMA BERENICES

That meant that these cocktails became more and more pointed at the situation of the masses—at Edie, at Mrs. Pogarski, at the space between her legs, at von Klunk. So the snowball got lost up ahead. It had succeeded in its mission, which was to put everybody out of doors for fifteen minutes. When they returned it was as though to a later act of the shabby costume drama in which all had become embedded like La Brea tar. There were new solutions wiggling to be applied and old ones which had been superseded though they lived on in the public consciousness like the memory of a beloved opera star and her tresses in a cell in the walls of an alveolate neo-gothic parlor. Fears that the snowball had reached extinction, or that it had been fatally sidetracked in the Coma Berenices of its own perverse self-projection through the dangerous daydreams of housewives, their hands at rest in the dishwater of a kitchen sink, or retirees and empty-nesters wishing to refinance the mortgage on their house or move to a smaller one or rent out part of it, proved premature. What piquantly captured the imagination of each, from competitor to consumer to straw boss to newly outsourced consultant, was how all-inclusive the bench warrant was. No beating about the bed of roses here!

Edie had felt vaguely apprehensive since the afternoon a dark-hatted man had called while she was out. He had said something about testing the water, her maid Maria told her. There had never been a problem with the water before. Maybe it was part of some ruse to get into the house and rummage around in Carl's papers. He hadn't called or returned. Yet she was left with the fact that he *had* been there; that something or someone wanted part of her attention; that is to say, part of her.

At five o'clock she mixed cocktails—for herself and Carl, should he show up—in the shaker old Mrs. Lavergne had left her. Bombay Sapphire martinis. Carl had fallen in love with them in Bangalore where he had been posted on an assignment. Somehow it was always a disappointment when they came out of the shaker colorless instead of blue. The sapphire color was in the bottle. She wondered if Carl had noticed this, or, more important, whether it bothered him. He had been so tight-lipped lately—though always the affectionate dear he had been on the day they first met at the Cayuga Country Club. Well, he'd had a lot on his mind. The refinancing hadn't been going too well—at least that was her impression, since he hadn't talked about it. When things went well he grew expansive, his tone avuncular. "Well, let's see what the pixies left in the larder last night. Maybe some little cheesie-biskies?"

The battlefront heat had been singeing everybody's nerves. Maria, badly off, had complained of backache. The arcane arousing had taken place on schedule. Then the arraignment was ascendant. The executive expectation, expecting expression, expectorated artwork, i.e., visual arts. The work of art had not arrived.

"Cut the mustard, curvaceous. This cutthroat-dance can't continue forever. I was downtown, saw your image enthroned above the city, through the grille, dilatory; apes and aphids continued pouring into the place. Soon we'll be looking at calmer quarters, a jar of moonshine reflecting the moon as in days gone by." Those were my sentiments too. Alas, Edie, we are no longer ourselves. Something came by and cut me down in the night. I was sure you'd notice. But the next day and the day after that came and went, and after that it was uncertain whether the observatory octet had finished

chiming beneath the liquid dome. We were all to blame. Collective guilt
is the only sure bet. But now I want you weaving in and out of my letter
to the editor, dated tomorrow. A Coromandel screen has patience only
with itself, but a quaff of grappa sees into and pierces the region of near
mists we know we know how to deal with.

The snowball is a model for the soul because billions of souls are
embedded in it, though none can dominate or even characterize it. In
this the snowball is like the humblest soul that ever walked the earth.
The rapacious, the raw, are its satellites. It wants you to believe its core
is the outermost shell of the universe, which may or may not be true.
Each of us has the choice of believing it, but we cannot believe in both
things without becoming separated from our core of enigma, which
soldiers on in good times and bad, protecting us alike from the
consequences of inaction and misguided enthusiasm. The snowball
would melt before it would release us from our vows.

After a mostly painful few years spent in Moscow (Idaho!), we changed to
Illinois. At first the cultural advantages of living in a large university
town were a boon, after the isolation we'd experienced. But gradually
harsher realities began to make themselves felt. A French film, an evening
at the ballet or a concert (mostly symphonic warhorses, like the 1812
Overture) every couple of months were hardly sufficient to keep reflections
on what we were missing out on in the big city from showing through the
threadbare drapes of our lives. The satin roof of our Colonial Revival house
looked fine from the street, but when you were under it you felt crushed
by the weight of the old twentieth century. The college radio station
emitted a perpetual flood of oldies or post-Schoenbergian twangs. Even

the book discussions ("round tables") seemed mostly aimed at a "young adult" audience. Mind you, neither Stu nor I have anything against the younger generation—we're not that far from it ourselves, kind of at the tail end of the baby-boom era. But so much serious attention brought to bear on subjects of doubtful consequence can get to you after a while. Many's the time we'd stare at each other across the living room and wonder, "So what?" Then one day a remarkable change occurred.

Some of us, quite a few, were fettered, many were not. The topiary Trojan horse stood outside the gate, not wanting to be let in. The free-lance were blue; the staff yellow. A stiff breeze was gathering itself in the west, indifferent to those who lay magnetized in its path or scurried to find some primitive shelter, a hollow log or overturned canoe. Jarvis and April, up to their necks in mimosa, could have cared less what intentions had etched themselves into the gigantic forehead that now loomed over all. A shrill fragrance, too aromatic for some, stood in the forward fields. I am benison, it sang; others may take heed or go back to their status as prisoners. But we, we all, are the stuff of legends, we urged. A quiet space for bathing, adorable beds that chase you into sleep, for dinner a dish of boiled puffin's eggs. Be careful, you'll disturb the pests, er, pets, April breathed. And if a few of them were released in time for tomorrow's match? Go, suffer with them. The carnage, the pandemonium go at it, as is their custom. Downstairs an old servant lurks, indifferent to minute changes in the wallpaper pattern, our unique heritage.

Today was nicer for a change. Marnie and Val are on their way to a trip through the New England states. In August, Merle stopped by "just to visit." We went to the new fish place and it was good. In February the two boys took me to the figure skating championships in Cincinnati, which I try never to miss. A month later we scrambled along the Carolina coast hoping for signs of spring. They were few and far between, mostly redbuds in bloom. Not a particularly attractive flower but one is grateful for any little swatch of color at that time of year. In late April and May the season kind of bottomed out. Too much rain. Evidence of copulation everywhere. I'm sure I missed a lot of the usual flowers of the spring, destroyed by the eccentric weather. At such times staying home can be a real blessing.

Summer was quiet except for the usual "transients." Fran and Don stopped by on their way to the traditional games in the Scottish highlands. They are centuries old and an amazing sight, it seems. Each sent a card from Scotland. Mary and her little boy came by in August. We went to the fish place but I'm not sure if Lance (her boy) appreciated it. Children have such pronounced tastes and can be quite stubborn about it. In late September a high point was the autumn foliage which was magnificent this year. Casper took me and his wife's two aunts on a "leaf-peeping" trip in northern Vermont. We were near Canada but didn't actually cross the border. You can get the same souvenir junk on this side for less money Max said. He is such a card.

November. Grief over Nancy Smith.

All in all this has been a fairly active and satisfying year, and I'm looking forward to the next one. Where it will take me I do not know. I just hang on and try to enjoy the ride. Snow brings winter memories. There is a warning somewhere in this but I do not know if it will be transmitted.

THE NEW HIGHER

You meant more than life to me. I lived through
you not knowing, not knowing I was living.
I learned that you called for me. I came to where
you were living, up a stair. There was no one there.
No one to appreciate me. The legality of it
upset a chair. Many times to celebrate
we were called together and where
we had been there was nothing there,
nothing that is anywhere. We passed obliquely,
leaving no stare. When the sun was done muttering,
in an optimistic way, it was time to leave that there.

Blithely passing in and out of where, blushing shyly
at the tag on the overcoat near the window where
the outside crept away, I put aside the there and now.
Now it was time to stumble anew,
blacking out when time came in the window.
There was not much of it left.
I laughed and put my hands shyly
across your eyes. Can you see now?
Yes I can see I am only in the where
where the blossoming stream takes off, under your window.
Go presently you said. Go from my window.
I am half in love with your window I cannot undermine
it, I said.

IN THOSE DAYS

Music, food, sex and their accompanying
tropes like a wall of light at a door
once spattered by laughter

come round to how *you* like it—
was it really you that approved?
And if so what does the loneliness
in all this mean? How blind are we?

We see a few feet into our future
of shrouded lots and ditches.
Surely that way was the long one
to have come. Yet nobody

sees anything wrong with what we're doing,
how we came to discuss it, here, with the wind
and the sun sometimes slanting.
You have arrived at this step, and the way down

is paralyzing, though this is the lost
youth I remember as being okay, once.
Got to shuffle, even if it's only the sarcasm
of speech that gets lost, while the blessed
sense of it bleeds through,

open to all kinds of interpretations.

A VISIT TO THE HOUSE OF FOOLS

The year subsides into clouds
more beautiful than any I have seen—
drifting equestrian statues, washing lifted by the wind.
Down here bodies made somber by the cold
meet and diverge at angles. Nothing is given
that may not be retracted. Our fires are glacial,
lighting up the polar backdrop. If you came it
would be in mid-parenthesis now, season of your engaging,
seminar not going anywhere. (I must wall these off;
nothing but a tree would pass here.)

There is no record that some of it was taken out
and later replaced in the file.
The cliff of windows, some lit up, some broken,
allows that variousness will attract
and repel, like a happy ending, the way the truth hurts.

How can "rare earth" be an element?

Test tubes doze. A wide window watches the sea.
Others blow inward toward the room with its floor
like an itch that scratching redeems.
A ruler is pasted against the wall
to tell time by, but it's too late. The snow's
knack for seeking out and penetrating crevices
has finally become major news.
Let's drink to that,
                    and the tenacity of just seeming.

DRYNESS OF MOUTH

NB: what is here is certainly not there,
nor are we apprenticed to an enchanter's doodling.
The pain of here contraindicates pleasant dreams of there,
though one could be forgiven for wishing things otherwise.

The alchemist put too much trust in his boy assistant,
who, while not vicious, was more alert than was called for,
notably when night whistled down the chimney
and the seven sisters cried out of their farandole:

"Desist! The time for ornery has lapsed,
and forgiveness and chilblains mingle on the horizon
of a doubt that can transform you." The lad, startled in mid-
apothegm, dropped his alembic. Uncomprehending love
spilled across the tundra, nothing there to dam it.

It was a situation he had oft dreamed as a tadpole:
uncomplicated kisses, stigmata strangely absent,
a field of violets shuddering. If it had to be this way,
better this way than a benediction signed by a reprieve.

Better the long way home, than home; better an unlit fire
than the frozen mantelpiece. Better toys than a blanket
of stars waiting for you upstairs. "Bankruptcy, ma'am: I'm
better at it than most. It definitely needs more salt."

INVOLUNTARY DESCRIPTION

That his landscape could have been the one you meant,
that it meant much to you, I never doubted,
even at the time. How many signifiers have you?
Good, I have two. I took my worries on the road
for a while. When we got back little cherubs were nesting
in the arbor, below the apple tree. We were incredulous,
and whistled. The road came back to get them
just as darkness was beginning.
The comic and the bathetic were our interior.
They kept integers at bay, and, when it was over,
toasted a little cheese to prove it never happened—
It had been reflected in a needle by the road's side.
The lovely sandlot was purple or gray.

Sometimes I think it's all one big affectation.
The forty jars, each holding its thief, draw closer
to me, trying to eavesdrop. But the only sound is water
dripping in the last millennium. I try and say it too;
you are glad it's over, except for a ton of sleep
and the half dreams that people it—people you knew,
but they weren't those people, only figures on a beach.

HÖLDERLIN MARGINALIA

for Anne Dunn

And in the soaking of which,
or the trunk.
is gas gas gas gas gas
    of which the room too
    is furnished

always the quaking of relief
is followed by gold scrub
piecings of a robot

They came to get you in times of relief as yet unimaginable,
or imagined—
circus tigers tip out on the loom, and the
    hand
    still stays.

An unseen servant stocks the kitchen with supplies
and our pantries are furbished by autumn
the kettle relinquishes nothing

———————————

Bye and bye
a grave overtook even the steamroller—what
        are you chanting at evening
        as evening's walls come together and break
He was my finest.
Lord the lingo the ingot
    feather that falls
    Secrets that brighten a night

The sand path to the open space
                            (in Maine)
and the lovers go under it is gaz
More gaz and gaz in the openings between the tombs.

Our hero arrives just in time
in "take charge" mode
        (feather that falls)
        (a silk stocking) (peed on) (in the autumn)
of bright nights
of favorable returns

_____

We who have
        had so much stamina it seems
impossible not to start again
        the cool, the water
everything is open
everything waits
this tree, this henhouse is open
or the aquarium lusts silently all an afternoon
for what images?
Billy the Kid
                try wry irises
                that is wiping the cataracts
                from them after they fold
                that is try anything, a sense of time is passing
        concerts that

_____

Out there on the golden sea   and other, more nets
            decided not to bring dawn yet not yet down
            the first big stairs

Then you grow up you grow away from
not meaning it as tedium—
everyone has to grow up a little in their life
a passion, orange,
platter of roses time will destabilize
in long or in large, keeps
still the secret.
The unfathomable is unfashionable
suited to ghost arguments
over what really did take place in the year mentioned—
was it over once it started? Nothing really was started
in that year or the next or the one after that.
Stranded in some hotel somewhere
the horizon looks out over meat
the prismatic colors of the tribes
avenged, assembling.
Peacock blue and black
Fig tree in terror to be assembling
its parsed fruits one by one or something
to the other
now it's past
            travel all night
            to the respected star
            fall and worship the pebble time left there

the eggs in the nest were brown, the veil too
                drawn
So why is five fingers the required figure
Who are you going to replace
nest egg
                and so it ought to be simple
                from a stork's-eye view
                set in bulbous hail perhaps we will rethink
                the bicycle came across the grass—
                "These are all pinups!"
                Class came to order
                the old order
                Class of '99
We should be growing in your pants
Think about it.

_____

One afternoon as golden stalks
grazed the parlor of heaven
the little shift in tone came
to tell us to get ready
to pack enough things
                The blue sky screeched
                A father and his daughter were passing
                the corner of the delighted crescent
Don't blame me for the stuff of change
        I too carry
        I think I'll go in now

The polar bear might travel hundreds of miles across the ice hunting for
food.

Its white fur is sometimes
used for clothes. Whose basket yawns
at the front door, under the eaves
giving little quarter to the stranger
giving up at last, at last given up.
O permanent thing,
in your recited lesson
plain as paper
modeled on the lawn,
                by someone,
                        and the whole
changes at last,
            is carried farther
                    than we wanted to be,
came undone,
            a padlock,
                unlucky
    for all the treatments, wobbly,
            and vague as trees,
                your unholy testaments
                    gathered to no purpose
                        ivy take note, and I
        right to the kill, the moment
            it takes, if it ever takes
            anything
                at all

———————

A vast rudeness all at once, blinking like an incredulous ocean
with its garters down, in the foam chest of thundering
purpose but in that case where is it
goes in with the hollyhock, that,
it now seems, always loved us,
without telling the truth but it scarcely matters.
There are still other stays to unfasten
linkage in the teeth of night,
                        both lion and tiger.
We blend in with one another.
The relief is in the book,
taken to new extremes,
to further sights
in the cause of a new dimension
growing back from the tree,
                        caused briefly
by someone's mistake
now sucked out like venom,
the tears of materiality, the skin
of the birch
blown away and within grace
                        divided.

TOLD HER TO GET ON WITH IT

At the pump, sticker shock reigned.
The lives of the residents were changed.

My head ached from those boulevards.
The distant bight
freezes over when it has to.

Flawed nourishment retracts like a feeler,
helicopters, penny lives
consigned to this pleasure as well—
I could see myself as a portion of malice
fading into the pollen of the grove.

The right of these citizens to keep silent:
cutting up things, bringing evidence, changing everything.

THE WEATHER, FOR EXAMPLE

Coasts are loud. Silences sin
at the meander of their doing.
All along the gatepost was wrong
as we suffered under that song,

wrong to shake the apron out
with crumbs the children marked
the way back with after it got dark.
Spoon the leaven in, there is more

to the hoods than flaps and strings.
A margin oozes.
It's Bakelite he said. I think it's Bakelite.
There's so much more we know,

time that wraps us in a swarm,
mongrels in nettle tilth,
percentages of doubt that shift unease,
bright locks along the shore.

I was once happy abed,
I could see it coming like a beach
then very fast. We are here to tell
some account of ourselves,

grab favor from the circumcised gods,
be replaced in a box or pocket.

Nothing coming from that quarter,
it behooveth the moth to inch back

against the steep Atlantic tides.
I found us here with toy fish,
choice clusters of whatever
you desired in time past,

rushing in to fill the unthinkable well.

AND COUNTING

The villa sat on a cone of volcanic rock high above a waveless sea that stretched away to a cloudless horizon. The sky, if that is what it was, was eggshell blue. The architecture melted into itself, so that what was decoration came to seem the fabric of the building, a rude, uncommunicative armature. Inside, many clocks were continually chiming and striking different hours. There was detail and some kind of curdled passion, not going very far, that evoked the negative way I feel about a job and such.

Pelleas wore a Santa Claus suit the color of faded columbine. I haven't looked at him in September. He hadn't done much to salvage the manners that snagged us, like seaweed caught in a ship's propeller. This abuse he's always heaping on me—I can't take it any more. Organ arpeggios gurgled down from the landing. Creative types in shorts have the option of sustaining the momentum or letting it collapse like a string of pearls on a cushion. She was instead dying for an eye operation. It was then I realized that I was part of the moving wall. Nothing could save us except the inevitable breaking of the text at the end of the chapter, a micro-redemption, like a green ray.

YOU SPOKE AS A CHILD

We sat together in the long hall.
There was something I'd wanted to ask you,
a new mood I was after. Something neither posed nor casual.
Outside under a slappy sky the leaves were right on.
They're our own skeletons. And slack was the tautology report.

They don't have bare beds. The children here are as
hunted rabbits, and don't think too much about what comes after.
A suffocated prince summons the septuor,
celestas wax dim and bright in the distance,
what was meant to be distance. You spoke out of the margin.

INTERESTING PEOPLE OF NEWFOUNDLAND

Newfoundland is, or was, full of interesting people.
Like Larry, who would make a fool of himself on street corners
for a nickel. There was the Russian who called himself
the Grand Duke, and who was said to be a real duke from somewhere,
and the woman who frequently accompanied him on his rounds.
Doc Hanks, the sawbones, was a real good surgeon
when he wasn't completely drunk, which was most of the time.
When only half drunk he could perform decent cranial surgery.
There was the blind man who never said anything
but produced spectral sounds on a musical saw.

There was Walsh's, with its fancy grocery department.
What a treat when Mother or Father
would take us down there, skidding over slippery snow
and ice, to be rewarded with a rare fig from somewhere.
They had teas from every country you could imagine
and hard little cakes from Scotland, rare sherries
and Madeiras to reward the aunts and uncles who came dancing.
On summer evenings in the eternal light it was a joy
just to be there and think. We took long rides
into the countryside, but were always stopped by some bog or other.
Then it was time to return home, which was OK with everybody,
each of them having discovered he or she could use a little shuteye.

In short there was a higher per capita percentage of interesting people
there than almost anywhere on earth, but the population was small,
which meant not too many interesting people. But for all that
we loved each other and had interesting times

picking each other's brain and drying nets on the wooden docks.
Always some more of us would come along. It is in the place
in the world in complete beauty, as none can gainsay,
I declare, and strong frontiers to collide with.
Worship of the chthonic powers may well happen there
but is seldom in evidence. We loved that too,
as we were a part of all that happened there, the evil and the good
and all the shades in between, happy to pipe up at roll call
or compete in the spelling bees. It was too much of a good thing
but at least it's over now. They are making a pageant out of it,
one of them told me. It's coming to a theater near you.

BROKEN TULIPS

A is walking through the streets of B, frantic
for C's touch but secretly relieved
not to have it. At Tamerlane
and East Tamerlane, he pauses, judicious:
The cave thing hasn't been seen again,
schoolgirls are prattling, and the Easter rabbit
is charging down the street, under full sail
and a strong headwind. Was ever anything
so delectable floated across the crescent moon's
transparent bay? Here shall we sit
and, dammit, talk about our trip
until the sky is again cold and gray.

Another's narrative supplants the crawling
stock-market quotes: Like all good things
life tends to go on too long, and when we smile
in mute annoyance, pauses for a moment.
Rains bathe the rainbow,
and the shape of night is an empty cylinder,
focused at us, urging its noncompliance
closer along the way we chose to go.

RETRO

It's really quite a thrill
when the moon rises above the hill
and you've gotten over someone
salty and mercurial, the only person you ever loved.

Walks in the park are enjoyed.
Going to Jerusalem now
I walked into a hotel room.
I didn't need a name or anything.
I went to Bellevue Hospital,
got a piece of the guy.
As I say, it's really quite a thrill.

Quite a thrill too to bend objects
that always return to their appointed grooves—
will it be always thus? Or will auto parts
get to have their day in the sun?

Got to drone now.
Princess Ida plans to overwork us four days a week
until the bracts have mauved up.
Then it's a tailgate party—
how would you like your burger done?

A little tea with that?

I saw her wailing for some animals.
That doesn't mean a thing doesn't happen

or only goes away, or gets worse.
What's the worst that could happen?

The midnight forest drags you along, thousands of peach hectares. Told
him I wouldn't do it if I was him. Nothing to halt the chatter of locusts
until they're put away for the night. He edges closer to your locker. Why
did I leave it open? I've forgotten the combination. But it seems he's not
interested in the locker, maybe my shoe—something unlike anything he's
ever known. Sensing the tension he broke the ice with a quip about the
weather somewhere, or maybe—maybe an observation on time, how it
moves vastly in different channels, always keeping up with itself, until the
day—I'm going to drive back to the office, a fellowship of miles, collect
some of last year's ammunition. Then I'm definitely going to the country,
he laughs.

CAPITAL O

Sweet food, I lap you up
as from a vessel of kindness.
We "unpack" paradigms of
unstructured mess. Leave us alone this day.

I'd like to write you about all this.
Similarly, I'd like not to have to write
about all the things we are
and never could be: the hereafter of things.

Or so it seemed, walking the plank
of every good thing
toward the tank of carnivorous eels
singing, chiming as we go

into subtracted Totentanz.
That is to say, behind
every good son
there is a watchful father.

Needless to tell, snow coughed up scenery.
There was a stop on the scenic railway
called Edelweiss, and as we got nearer
my heart began to sing lighter,

I was approached by foreign agents
masquerading as talent scouts

and lo, everything dissolved became grand;
there were blind lanterns in the sedge

and the shimmy was named dance of the year.
Soon, the deadline had been passed,
meaning new lime-green shoots in the distance
and banqueting on the firing range

where all reaction is overdue
and the stars shudder and turn silver,
then pink in the difficult light.
Then it's tomorrow and breakfast,

with unanswered letters galore, and this page,
this furtive one, tucked out of an envelope
please, let there be more commotion,
less avian flu. I mean, even cats
are aware, even as they prowl, which is much the same

while you and I pierced the lotus
and the old stereopticon came apart
in my hands, reward for sub rosa being.

ANNUALS AND PERENNIALS

Telling it so simple, so far away,
as this America, home of the free,
colored ashes smeared on the base
or pedestal that flourishes ways of doubting
to be graceful, wave a slender hand . . .

We are fleet and persecuting
as hawks or crows.
We suffer for the lies we told, not wanting to
yet cupped in the wristlock of grace,
teenage Borgias or Gonzagas,
gold against gray in bands streaming,
meaning no harm, we never

meant it to, this stream that outpours now
haplessly into the vestibule that awaits.

We have shapes but no power.

WOLF RIDGE

Attention, shoppers. From within the inverted
commas of a strambotto, seditious whispering
watermarks this time of day. Time to get out
and, as they say, about. Becalmed on a sea
of inner stress, sheltered from cold northern breezes,
idly we groove: Must have
been the time before this, when we all moved
in schools, a finny tribe, and this way
and that the caucus raised its din:
punctuation and quips, an "environment"
like a lovely shed. My own plastic sturgeon
warned me away from knowing. Now look at the damage.
You can't. It's invisible. Anyway, you spent his love,
swallowed everything with his knives,
a necessary unpleasantness viewed from the rumble seat
of what was roaring ahead.

I want to change all that.
We came here with a mandate of sorts, anyway
a clear conscience. Attrition and court costs
brought you last year's ten best. Now it's firm
and not a bit transparent. Everybody got lost
playing hide-and-seek, except you,
who were alone. Not a bad way to end the evening,
whistling. They wanted a bad dinner,
and at this time a bad dinner was late.
Meatloaf, you remembered, is the third vegetable.

WHEN I SAW THE INVIDIOUS FLARE

When I saw the invidious flare
and houses rising up over the horizon
I called to my brother. "Brother," I called,
"why are these chameleons teasing us?
Is it that they are warthogs, and the gamekeeper is napping?
What I'd give for a pint of English bitter,
or anything, practically anything at all.
How lonesome it seems when you're choosing,
and then, when you have done so, it seems even more lonesome.
We should have got out more during the last fine days.
Now, love is but a lesson, and a tedious one at that.
Do they think they can expel me from this school, or, worse,
suspend me? In which case all my learning will be as straw,
though there'll be a lot of it,
I can assure you."

Evening waves slap rudely at the pilings
and birds are more numerous than usual.
There are some who find me sloppy, others
for whom I seem too well-groomed. I'd like to strike
a happy medium, but style
is such a personal thing, an everlasting riddle.

Then I saw the flare turn again.
Help, it said, I want to get out of this
even more than you do. I was once a fair twinkling light
at the end of a tunnel, then someone wished this on me.
Help me to put it behind me please.

Turning from the blaze to the counterpane
I saw how we are all great in our shortcomings, yea,
greater because of them. There are letters in the alphabet
we don't know yet, but when we've reached them
we'll know the luster of unsupported things.
Our negativity will have caught up with us
and we'll be better for it. Just
keep turning on lights, wasting electricity,
carousing with aardvarks, smashing the stemware.
These apartments we live in are nicer
than where we lived before, near the beginning.

HEAVY HOME

. . . hungry eaters of a slender substance
—C. M. DOUGHTY

One thing follows another awning in the event horizon. One life in the
going changes the subject. Some things made sense, others didn't. I
didn't expect to die so soon. Well, I guess I'll have to have tabulated
myself in some way. I'd discussed writing on your leg. Others in the
tree school groaned, stirred in their sleep, having lately put away
childish things. All of us late. What if we lived overseas? We could
survive on alms and pledges for a while, find jobs in the barrel industry,
decoct melismas on which to build an echo.

Here we break camp; it was decreed by an elder, or alder. He put the
water on to boil. He sends us itches and the wherewithal to scratch
them, fossils in the guise of party favors. Then sprang dull-headed
into the gilded surround, chimera after all. Tears from the doll leaked
out. It was as if we had chosen this path on a different journey, and
were waiting in the deafening wilderness for our instincts to catch up,
leggy hope.

Many flushings of the toilet later you'll give it back and we'll give it
to the mechanical oracle, render unto caesura, and expect thrifty
thanks, somewhere between laughter and obloquy. But how quaint the
semicircular drive and its trimmings: gazing globe, lark's mirror, lime
twigs, tinsel, ormolu, Venus's-flytrap, *pattes de velours,* Rembrandt and
his goat. On a return visit we were not received, the grace period
having expired.

The pictograph is also a chimera. Since day one you've abused it. Resting on our oars we breathe in the attar of dissent, breaking off of negotiations, recall of ambassadors, the rift within the lute. For the time being the disputed enclave is yours. But its cadence is elsewhere.

THE SITUATION UPSTAIRS

Like a forest fire in a jungle
with no one to watch it, this sea breeze
releases me to the cloud of knowing.

There are beaters in the woods,
nourishing it, and you're it,
reciting it. The long scramble upstairs
landed us here. There is no method
in the alphabet; the urchin was unseated.

You have to learn to "bounce"
with the ages, just to keep up with time.
By then it will have been censored,
bleached from an autumn of discord.
In time we were twins, grew apart,
felt the centennial dawning.
There was nowhere to turn
and nobody to turn to.

To have "landed" requires skills
we knew nothing of in our era,
yet their musicianly acts accompany us,
push us out of doors, into late summer's clamor,

where our pleated longevity mimics us.
We should have been nicer, talked to children
and their pets. To draw the tapestry aside
at this late date is to shuffle with fools

and clergymen, though there is one more thankless
task to claim and be influenced by:
the credible flight of footfall plays and calls.

These not any more for our adornment:
talking to new rulers and insight gained,
sunflowers over and out,
ashes on the clapboard credenza.

WELL-LIT PLACES

The horse chestnut tree shelters the house of princes.
The laurel nudges the catalpa.
Mussolini offers a diamond to Corot.
The proud, the famous, the magnificent
exude gentleness and megalomania.
Embassies are loud with the sound of cymbals and organ.
The taste of insolence is sharp, with an agreeable mingled sweetness.

A man declaiming in front of a coat of arms
is possessed of great pride and believes no man equal to himself in valor,
      dignity or competence.
He will have two wives who will love him dearly and whom he won't love at all.
He will be irascible and lustful.
He will endure many reverses because of his sudden wrath and his great courage.

The girl will have a large and wide bosom.
She will experience disappointment at the age of twelve through an act of
      oppression or virginal corruption.
She will conquer in all things, with God's help and that of the fuchsia, the
      orange, and the dahlia.

MEANINGFUL LOVE

What the bad news was
became apparent too late
for us to do anything good about it.

I was offered no urgent dreaming,
didn't need a name or anything.
Everything was taken care of.

In the medium-size city of my awareness
voles are building colossi.
The blue room is over there.

He put out no feelers.
The day was all as one to him.
Some days he never leaves his room
and those are the best days,
by far.

There were morose gardens farther down the slope,
anthills that looked like they belonged there.
The sausages were undercooked,
the wine too cold, the bread molten.
Who said to bring sweaters?
The climate's not that dependable.

The Atlantic crawled slowly to the left
pinning a message on the unbound golden hair of sleeping maidens,
a ruse for next time,

where fire and water are rampant in the streets,
the gate closed—no visitors today
or any evident heartbeat.

I got rid of the book of fairy tales,
pawned my old car, bought a ticket to the funhouse,
found myself back here at six o'clock,
pondering "possible side effects."

There was no harm in loving then,
no certain good either. But love was loving servants
or bosses. No straight road issuing from it.
Leaves around the door are penciled losses.
Twenty years to fix it.
Asters bloom one way or another.

MORE FEEDBACK

The passionate are immobilized.
The case-hardened undulate over walls
of the library, in more or less expressive poses.
The equinox again, not knowing
whether to put the car in reverse
or slam on the brakes at the entrance
to the little alley. Seasons belong
to others than us. Our work keeps us
up late nights; there is no more joy
or sorrow than in what work gives.
A little boy thought the raven on the bluff
was a winged instrument; there is so little
that gives and says it gives. Others
felt themselves ostracized by the moon.
The pure joy of daily living became impacted
with the blood of fate and battles.
There's no turning back the man says,
the one waiting to take tickets at the top
of the gangplank. Still, in the past
we could always wait a little. Indeed,
we are waiting now. That's what happens.

LOST FOOTAGE

You said, "Life's a hungry desert,"
or something like that. I couldn't hear.

The curving path escorts us
to Armida's pavilion. The enchantress.
She had everything built slightly smaller
than life size, as you'll find
if you sit in the chair at that table.

And clean—everything is terribly clean,
from the crumbs casting long shadows
on the breadboard, to the gnats churning in the open window.

We can't mask the anxiety for long,
but we can produce good and cherishable deeds
to be ransacked by those who come after us.
True, no one visits anymore.
I used to think it was because of him, now
I think it's because of him and us.

We grow more fragile at our posts,
interrogating vacant night. "Who goes there?"
And he goes, "Nay, stand and unfurl yourself."

I thought, in the corner, in the canyon,
in the cupboard, was something that seized me
in a terrible but approachable embrace.

All was silent except the pedals
of the loom, from which a tapestry streams
in bits and pieces. "I don't care how you do it."

I can see the subject: an eagle with Ganymede
in his razor-clam claws, against a sky
of mottled sun and storm clouds.

From that, much vexation.

THE RED EASEL

Say doc, those swags are of the wrong period
though in harmony with the whole. You shouldn't take it too hard.
Everybody likes it when the casual drift
becomes more insistent, setting in order the house
while writing finis to its three-decker novel. Only when the plaint
of hens pierces dusk like a screen door
does the omnipresent turn top-heavy. Oh, really?
I thought they had names for guys like you
and places to take them to. That's true, but
let's not be hasty, shall we, and pronounce your example
a fraud before all the returns are in? These are,
it turns out, passionate and involving, as well as here to stay.

NOVELTY LOVE TROT

I enjoy biographies and bibliographies,
and cultural studies. As for music, my tastes
run to Liszt's Consolations, especially the flatter ones,
though I've never been consoled
by them. Well, once maybe.

As for religion, it's about going to hell,
isn't it? I read that 30 percent of Americans believe in hell,
though only one percent thinks they'll end up there,
which says a lot about us, and about the other religions.
Nobody believes in heaven. Hell is what gets them fired up.
I'm probably the only American

who thinks he's going to heaven, though my reasons
would be hard to explain. I enjoy seasons
and picnicking. A waft from a tree branch
and I'm in heaven, though not literally.
For that one must await the steep decline
into a declivity, and shouts from companions
who are not far off.

In the end it matters little what things we enjoy.
We list them, and barely have we begun
when the listener's attention has turned to something else.
"Did you *see* that? The way that guy cut him off?"
Darlings, we'll all be known for some detail,
some nick in the chiseled brow, but it won't weigh much
in the scale's careening pan. What others think

of us is the only thing that matters,
to us and to them. You are stuffing squash blossoms
with porcini mushrooms. I am somewhere else, alone as usual.

I must get back to my elegy.

THE TEMPLATE

was always there, its existence seldom
questioned or suspected. The poets of the future
would avoid it, as we had. An imaginary railing
disappeared into the forest. It was here that the old gang
used to gather and swap stories. It
was like the Amazon, but on a much smaller scale.

Afterwards, when some of us swept out into the world
and could make comparisons, the fuss seemed justified.
No two poets ever agreed on anything, and that amused us.
It seemed good, the clotted darkness that came every day.

FROM CHINA TO PERU

I was taunted for wearing a dark woollen suit to the occasion, or
"affair," though most of the others were similarly dressed, including my
tormentor. True, it was autumn and darkness had fallen quite early,
though there was a sultriness like that of summer in the air. I would
have been happy to change into something lighter, both as to weight
and color—something "natural." But there was no time, or place, in
addition to the lack of suitable attire, if that's what it would have been,
since the mass of dark clothes had taken on a kind of accusatory mien.
Men who looked as though they were about to go off on safari or had
just returned from one were downing Jell-O shots. To do this it seemed
to be necessary to walk backward to a corner of the room shrouded in
potted palms, then lurch ataxically toward the bar where the required
drink was presented silently and as silently consumed. Sometimes one
could hear the soft, laughing chatter of little girls in the distance (what
distance? the room was fairly small), which seemed like applause for an
act performed several minutes ago. It was unnerving—like a circus. I
understood the meaning of the phrase "three-ring circus"—something
where you see only a partial arc of several events, segments that are
supposed to add up to something much less than the sum of their parts,
something purposely deficient in meaning. I was thirsty for the cocktail
hour that would undoubtedly follow this strange competition.

Then the unthinkable happened—it all began to break up like the first
wave of a retreating tide on a rock in the sea. In less than half a minute
the sea had completely withdrawn, leaving a startled landscape of reefs
and crowds, fierce and bristling as the water danced away from them.
These were my coevals. They were still dressed like me, or rather, I like
them. A draught from an opened window crawled through the

apartment, rustling papers and the leaves of plants. A sheet of newsprint slid toward me in jerks and feints—two steps forward, one step back—until finally I could read the headline: "Japan Declares War on Austro-Hungary. Siamese Ambassador Recalled."

I would have been happy with a weather report. But though some of the girls tried, there was no way of getting it to me. Full of remorse, I sank down on a footstool and soon forgot all the horror of my situation.

IDEA OF THE FOREST

I enjoy all this emerging, holding of hands—
what isn't better than holding hands? For we get to see
into the distance, far from ways others carved,
even a little reality, darker intake
though there was a shadow brain in their regular nipples
as the auto thought to stop. I'll bring the devilled eggs.
Sincere messages are my form of expression.
Follow the giant home but don't let him see you. Remember
the grass will always let you out. Just don't *steal* out.

THE INJURED PARTY

This one knows;
this one went hence like a conversion
as Chopin played in their living rooms
and bats tilted through the long summer.

Making love to the cement, a dropout
had seen sheaves before.
The appeal wound its way through the courts,
pausing, now and then, for a drink of water,
ending in a "stale mate."

And for a number of years, our track record
was zero and polite. Those who remembered us at all
were amazed to be greeting us this side of heaven.
We fidgeted with our hair, pleaded with the presiding judge,
but the end was my initials, and the date, carved in roman numerals.
Oh, I see. You're here of those who love us.
The others are outside.
The wind is blowing.

We paint the word "winter" on the door.

A DARNING EGG

He had emerged from the woods. Two poachers fired their rifles above his head. He couldn't restrain his joy.

He danced with the cypress, and stopped.

Cancel the order. The choir of aging starlets that blundered halfway through here tonight shrugged, appalled probably. Wasn't it time to go? Wearily they turned back down the cobalt and terra-cotta ramp, singing a song to hoist their spirits, the "Marche Militaire." Now eyeballs close on the distant porousness. It's not liquor that gets us there.

Think tiny and big, the "experiment perilous."

Evelyn surveyed the shadow. Later, he'd see.

And the heavens, it was all duty after that. Duty calls. Which isn't to say pleasure doesn't too, and louder. My head is so screwed up I can't find your name in the yearbook. Years ago, it was like mist.

The cat is trained to touch base, scout out new locations. We'll all be back in a year's time, to the day. We'll see how it looks then. Meantime grades and awards are to be given out. Sheepskin hung on the walls in brocaded taverns. It was all over for them. But like them, a kiss comes to light our way in the eccentric competition.

Remember that I loved you. See no more.

WILD CITY

On the dust bed the frequency of the oscillations is rapidly becoming untenable. Make that amenable. Oh, and if anyone calls tell them I've gone out to lunch, which, in fact, I have.

Their anniversary turned back into bed. One day on our pollen chart I notice the spots of autumn are getting larger. The light is that self-confident yellow. I hear there's no perspective where you're going. That populous "upstate" of dogs and ponies. Why make a picture then? Nobody said you had to brook rabble. A little fretful calm is sweeter than shrouded peaks, large birthday celebrations of the new neighbor no one knows yet.

Good to get back to the queer stuff after so unstable an interregnum, and we fed the poor just as it says here somewhere we're supposed to, but who knew how ravenous they can get! Heeded at night, they go on for a while as programmed, until it becomes glaringly evident that the beginning has collapsed and the serried ranks above are leaning together for support, glazed by the wind. Go, dummy, and ask for ice cream, chocolate and vanilla, and a mechanic if they have one. My crankcase needs asperging.

While the trees were there a new and angry god took over. Pass the sugar tongs. It was just like it was going to be when it was over, yet still a lively sense of being barely halfway there in the sunny beams did glide. Weigh his parchment carefully.

Then lo, I love more than one, which is impossible, unless the whisper of wine itself susurrate otherwise, in which case I agree to everything.

Here, let's sign a treaty, or tear one up, and the eradication of borders will guide us more faithfully to the customhouse. An angel on a dime casts an inquiring glance in our direction. Sure honey, you can ride for free. We're all going in the same direction. But I have to go back and get something I left in the cast-iron drugstore.

THE BLED WEASEL

Two shoes make a difference
to the man in the street. The detention of the Magna Carta
was forever but it's over now.
Three Greek youths pass. "Have a good one."
And I, contorted as I am . . .
First I repaired to the almshouse,
then to a nearby distillery. Sure and if it ain't
the baby's comic death, we'll come no more
nor promise what we had seen.

Erect on its parasol
the caterpillar predicted three more months of gloom.
Chatty figures lurked about. There was nothing
much anyone could do. We spread jam on it
which helped, but only a little. More ogres from the other side
crossed over to ours. Glowworms circulated
under the trees, confirmed by whimpering Dobermans, yet
all was somehow lightness and ease. The wealth of nations
floated into our laps, as though there had never been a housing crisis,
or as if we, all of us, had invented a kind of shelter
unmentioned in the glossy manuals.
The ark is a type of tree, you said, and he breathed
fury into my face. That was in the time when it was just as well
to be, having been, and all the vagrant notions of our past
collapsed in a crazy quilt of expired pageantry.

A BELOW-PAR STAR

After the shouting in the wilderness
and the colors that don't quite match, and shouldn't,
behold I handle you, mournful love,
like a scene in a cigarette pageant.

Your face is as white as linen on a board.
I pray that the skies will soak up your electricity,
the birds founder and come to heel,
the drive-by stabbings evaporate into friendly if noncommittal steam,

and tragedy draw his petticoat across your face
because it doesn't happen enough.
A lifeboat almost swamped by shrugs, your famous kisser
now floats over all American cities like a *drapeau*.

They said you'd be here sooner. It's still early, but I can wait
no longer. It's bed and the movies for me.
Tomorrow, exceptionally, there may be a flawed native pearl for breakfast,
and in October, lots of weather, much of it cruder.

THE SNOW-STAINED PETALS AREN'T
PRETTY ANY MORE

A chance encounter in the street, an ancient phrase offered by a delicate woman, sends him back to burrow in the rubble of his youth. A few viable wisps still protrude. It all involves fetishes, those poor misunderstood employees of the sexual closet. Despised worker bees. Those bondsmen are in town, bonding. And what shall I tell the sales representative when he calls? That we don't need any fireworks. We're living backward. We're not making up for the mistakes of the past, we are the past.

He was sinking into a kind of lethargic kick the house had never seen him in. And was hiding in one. You, always so good at the old days when something you do for the young ladies comes up again in conversation, can you still conjugate? The gray parrot stretches his alarming scarlet wing, and the room falls silent, save for the hastily indrawn breath of a few of the participants. It's four o'clock, you've come late, that wraps up nap time. The old fake dilemma, not urgent. I've even forgotten it, so go on with your story. Man walks into bar. Stilled avalanches back up, in slow motion. White snow on dun cement. For the seasons to withdraw, cherries must first come alive, in a burst of somewhat embarrassing frankness, while the distant rumble goes on: the opportunity for something to do something else, for it to be something else. Meanwhile, the Hardys ride high. Why? They didn't send the blotch to me, the postmark is missing. And the stamp? All colliding, twisting like train smoke in the wind, rattled by the elements. To punish people after dark. Buster issued a warning. In the shape of a message in a bottle, cast into the sea off the Cape of Good Hope. When his sister found it some twelve years later all his prognostications had come true, yet they hadn't mattered much. No one had paid attention. Such, my friends, is the reward of study and laborious attempts to communicate with the dead. In the end it all falls to pieces.

TENSION IN THE ROCKS

They changed for dinner. In those days
no one was in a hurry, it was real time
every time. Usually the streets were saddled with fog
at night. In the daytime it mostly blew away.
We kept on living because we knew how.
Maple seeds like paperclips skittered in the *allées*.
We knew not how many enthusiasts climbed the slope,
nor how long they took. It was, in the words of one,
"beholding" not to know. We eased by.

You can see how the past has come to pass
in the ferns and sweepings of ore and text
that shadowed such narratives as had been scratched,
as though any hotel guest could wipe the blight away
and in so doing, be redeemed for the moment.
I tell you it was not unseemly.
Little girls gathered in groves to see the wish spelled out,
yet under the hemlocks all was moulting, a fury
of notations, obliterated. We knew who to thank
for the postcard. It was signed, "Love, Harold and Olive."

COUNTERPANE

Ma chambre a la forme d'une cage
—APOLLINAIRE

One might as well pick up the pieces.
What else are they for? And interrupt someone's organ recital—
we *are* interruptions, aren't we? I mean in the highest sense
of a target, welcoming all the dust and noise
as though we were the city's apron.

Going out has another factor about it—
the mineral salts that have leached through our wall
staining it untoward colors, yet we wait
for them, the peace goes on in our mouth.

Sometimes suicide seems like a neat solution—
"elegant," as mathematicians say,
and it's too late to be counted out.
But the black tide mounting in us is probably the best

method. It makes you want to exercise
and simultaneously gasp, give up resting
and spend a little time with a book, or encourage the vine to grow.
We'll need all the feelers we can get come December,

so go on putting them out. Operators are waiting to take your call,
overloaded trunk lines bawling regret,
yet the one answer, when it comes, isn't particularly cogent,
though it means well, inviting us to rest on sparse laurels

and drilling a little fancy into the brain next door.
"How's about it, Chief? Gotten in any smooth ones yet?"
That wisteria sky has to become a sea of comfort
on which we're cut adrift with lots of friendly goats and ghosts.

Life is a warehouse sale for the initiated,
i.e., those who know where to go and find it,
then make it back to the abandoned comb
we've thought about so intensely across the spruced-up years.

TWO MILLION VIOLATORS

Like a hair falling on sand
the return address is emptiness
or openness,
whichever way that leads us,
makes us happen.

Stars shift in their sockets.
God patrols the bottom of the sea,
lifts the doric snails
to fire-escape level.
Sees us coming
and turns a corner.

Pasteboard men idle in their shops
past the gliding hour,
serve us tea and sherbets
conniving in the small back room.

We have filled these orders
over and over, it says,
exported our waste
to the furthest reaches of the empire.
Still no singsong,
bird jangle in the ears.

Still no ermine slope
fanning downward,
nor eyrie for the mind.
Distressed stone terraces contain
all the abatement.

SONNET: MORE OF SAME

Try to avoid the pattern that has been avoided,
the avoidance pattern. It's not as easy as it looks:
The herringbone is floating eagerly up
from the herring to become parquet. Or whatever suits it.
New fractals clamor to be identical
to their sisters. Half of them succeed. The others
go on to be Provençal floral prints some sleepy but ingenious
weaver created halfway through the eighteenth century,
and they never came to life until now.

It's like practicing a scale: at once different and never the same.
Ask not why we do these things. Ask why we find them meaningful.
Ask the cuckoo transfixed in mid-flight
between the pagoda and the hermit's rococo cave. He may tell you.

THE LOVE INTEREST

We could see it coming from forever,
then it was simply here, parallel
to the day's walking. By then it was we
who had disappeared, into the tunnel of a book.

Rising late at night, we join the current
of tomorrow's news. Why not? Unlike
some others, we haven't anything to ask for
or borrow. We're just pieces of solid geometry:

cylinders or rhomboids. A certain satisfaction
has been granted us. Sure, we keep coming back
for more—that's part of the "human" aspect
of the parade. And there are darker regions

penciled in, that we should explore some time.
For now it's enough that this day is over.
It brought its load of freshness, dropped it off
and left. As for us, we're still here, aren't we?

COMPOSITION

We used to call it the boob tube,
but I guess they don't use tubes anymore.
Whatever, it serves a small purpose after waking
and before falling asleep. Today's news—
but is there such a thing as news,
or even oral history? Yes, when you want to go back
after a while and appraise the accumulation
of leaves, say in a sandbox.
The rest is rented depression,
available only in season
and the season is always next month,
a pure but troubled time.

That's why I don't go out much, though
staying at home never seemed much of an option.
And speaking of nutty concepts, surely "home"
is way up there on the list. I feel more certain about "now"
and "then," because they are close to me,
like lovers, though apparently not in love with me,
as I am with them. I like to call to them,
and sometimes they reply, out of the deep business of some dream.

LIKE MOST SEAS

The cellos offer appropriate pithy fare
to the violas, who aspire to something higher,
not, as it turns out, on the map. We walk the familiar avenue
into the city, and a few raindrops
tickle the leaves overhead. Down here it is mostly dry
and unserious. On disputed ground right now
truant officers pronounce the schools sound. Yay!
And the dog catcher has announced his retirement
by the end of August. Spaced not too far
from each other, the bridges resemble eyeglasses.
Space needles lean into the breeze.

Just this far it happened, on another day:
Mothers gave notice, their kids a seething conundrum
of black-out jokes and memory passages.
Not all of us were being let in, and the portcullis
seemed to take a distinct relish in spearing
the most rumpled and least distinguished, though there was no question
of justice; the caretaker government had been abolished back in winter.
Slander was acceptable and as lighthearted
as comments on one's pachysandra or the new tax rolls.
We could hear the gargle of the sea from a great distance.
Soon it would be lapping at the attics of the poor
and the high-flown terraces of the rich.
No one thought about leaving, or rather it was moving
that no one thought about. We were each happy in the cell
of our self-determination, attentively falling out of love
with the atrium of tomorrow, its muscle, its bravado.

NEW CONCERNS

Sulfurous, Mrs. Hanratty's apron floats
above the sunset, auguring extreme cold.
The guests' advantage doesn't undermine
their green goalie days.

Wind-driven pea shoots strew the skies.
All is tremor, modesty, a waiting to be told.
Several speakers impugn at once
the veracity of a late brook in August,
and all it would have meant on the same day
in another year. By now, runners will have reached
the northern border, plunged fingertips
in the flame. And, yes,

this is one of those times.

THE LOST TRAIN

Understanding all, our dreams are important, in that they tell us
what we must not do to stay awake.

Patience is nothing to write home about.

Call me choosy, I enjoy seeing a gunboat in the harbor, it signals me
we can always turn back to sip the past once it's over. The miracle-wracked
strand appreciates a breather, a sigh brought forth on the lips. Reading
testimony to Eskimos.

Dreams can strike in your sleep when you are least aware of it.

She lacked the political savvy to go far in this disgruntled universe.

One other time when I was half turned around, I saw it coming and forgot
to duck. That was not much of a time though, larding the zipper till
the trough fell out and the west wind bloomed reasonably. The others were
in housewares, in full cry, all mattress points north.

Darting up a hair ladder the moon triumphs over a least twitch.

IN THE TIME OF CHERRIES

Is it raining yet? I quit. The bands of motivation
recede, in intensity, like paint chips—
heavy to pale. It is acknowledged
that this is the strength of things,

that they will not get better.
One day things actually were better.
It was a season in time, muffled in song.
We liked standing at the edge of it,
imagining the wonderful things that could be here,
and that they are here, which is much the same.

Shy time that dives into the wings,
too embarrassed to acknowledge the applause,
dense, like a runnel attacking.

In another age of soda fountains and running boards
it hadn't mattered. Now it was reduced to a bright
particular atom, deep blue and exemplary.

For you, seduction was a way of accelerating,
though not catching up, like Atalanta's run.
The apples were added by a later source.
Call it pagan, i.e., traceless. Call me
irresponsible, I'll be back in August,
after the cherries have left.
How motivated is that?

WHERE SHALL I WANDER

Shifting, too anxious to be fully aware, the screen of dirt and glitter grazes the edge of the pavement. It is understood that this is now the past, sixty, sixty-four years ago. It matters precisely at the drip of blood forming at the end of an icicle that hisses at you, you're a pod of a man. You know, forget and dislike him.

The row of dishes stretched into the distance, dreaming. Is it Japan where you are? Who are these slate prisons, aligned, half bowing offstage, half erupting out of the prompter's box? Glycerin stains the cheeks

and the old fire tongs have their say. This is a story in a chest. Conversations at night not meant to be overheard, so you can't tell exactly when you came in, at which second. The interior is meant to be homey upstairs, downstairs, all across the hall, dazzled from the blue microsecond it took to get here, but if then, why? Why the commotion on the shore? Traces of birds in the sand, birdshit, claw marks. And the rest are missing.

Soon bread will announce itself. To be seen from behind, here is what you have to do. Smear a tongue depressor with a little suet, then stand away, pessimistic as always. The part in your hair will come to seem the natural one. Your faded red T-shirt is indeed ours to look at. Except there are too many middle-aged rubes now. You know, you've got to go out, jostle the barometer, bump into the hall tree and excuse yourself, descend three steps, walk to the curb and pee against someone's sedan. Then it may turn out that you have seen *your* back. A joyful roar lit up the headlands, from afar screeching white as the World's Columbian Exposition, inspiration to architects of the burgeoning Twentieth Century, swarming now, too hungry to appease, let's get on with it. But you have to do it more often. To qualify for some of that relief aid. Kings in their dungeons applaud the new centennial, McKinley assassinated. Lake Erie broods, pushes its lower lip out. OK, if you can get all you want through mismanagement, this late-breaking trust buster can do the same, providing you all shape up. Mansions and factories line Dakota Boulevard. Skyboards, and the dark rhythms of houses, shuttered, forever, what concept is that? In the end the jazz reaches will effort it out. Darn it,

I like your lingo. We two be here all the same. The Russian sparrows wheel pesteringly, no it is not time to come in, I said no it is not a time to come in. Fine we'll stay out where it's mild,

contingency is all the rage here. I said . . . No but there comes a time when contingency itself is contingent on the abrupt desire to happen, a colossal burp brewing somewhere. And moreover what I maintained to you once stands, signpost in the desert pointing the wrong way, we'll get back whatever way we can, sure as heck. Then you just came around the barn's edge as though materializing, it wouldn't have taken much. So why didn't I . . . didn't we . . . It's past time, half past time, too late but another time, so long, so long for a while, geez I don't know, the answer, if I did, you—and if I did . . .

Effably, it talks on, not paring it, scrambled then restructured, a song to remember in reckless sleep, bygones. She used to say, "as Amy would say, as Leon would say," and let this stand as a portal cut into the granite face, from which one could view shards within, boulders tormented as though by torrents, but still, as though motion had never dreamed of sleep. Then to stand up and stretch, the day draining. Scratch any itch, the somber legato underneath will surge prominently, lean on the right lever. Absence

relieves itself, got to be getting on with those notes. Let's see . . . Wherever a tisket is available, substitute an item from column B, then return to the starting goal. The challenger barely had time to mouth our initials, the glaze was off the cake, whoa, before there were few but now they are all of a piece, snoring to drown the freesia's reticence. Charles is gone. He used to live here, when blood erupted into riots and the frugal demurrers retreated all of a sudden. We like to use to be here, scrubbing soap stone, celebrating rags in my head to make the antlers glow. Use medium strength bleach until pursued clobbered effect pulsates in little burrs, grace notes in an awful cataract, groans we anticipated, revelers' premature hoo-ha. Grouchy he acceded, a jobber's whisk

parses the banished interval. But why talk of housebreaking on a night like this? To one viewer, off in different directions with elaborate casualness, to regroup behind Rusty's garage, concocting who knows what deviltry, having conveniently evaporated from the hoary scribe's all-consuming minutes. And if you were to tape the *remous* famously issuing from the ensuing gaggle—would you do it differently? For time, and this is where it gets really nasty, remembers all of us, recognizes us making allowances for our changed appearance and greets us familiarly by name, only occasionally getting mixed up (though it does happen). So who's to blame us for signing off on our agenda and sinking into a cozy chair, accepting the proffered sherry and sighing for a time when things really were easier and more people were alive. That, and Jack's tattoo. But there was something else slinking up via the back way and mingling with the invited guests, *mine de rien*. Not a bailiff or a rejected suitor from prelapsarian school picnics, nor yet a seemingly indifferent observer, tie-clasp camera getting it all down, nor a truly open-minded member of the cultivated bourgeoisie our grandfathers sprang from or knew about, but a cosmic dunce, bent on mischief and good works with equal zest, somebody fully determined to *be* and not disturb others with his passive-aggressive version of how things are and ever shall be—the distinguished visiting lecturer.

Smack in the limousine, the friendly fog next door placed a hand on my shoulder, cementing matters. The professor looked wary. "Flowers have helped pave roads," he mooted. The ocean filling in for us. Too many vacant noon empires, without them you can't rule a hemisphere or be sated other than by watching. Our TV brains sit around us all brave and friendly, like docile pets. We get by by tweaking. Seems it's always going on in another's head, far from the painted asters and the glorious headlands of Maine, far from everything you could just about entertain. Was that you sermonizing? Go right ahead, be my guest. I'll sit here in the blue room till it's time, cradling my wrists in my shawl. But I wish to be remembered, if only by you. Make it stick.

Oh, *that* traveling salesman. And, enthused, I bought away from the long procession of vowels in pajamas. It was as though I and the world didn't matter. And thick the birds plowed the air, as though driven by an intimate force like that which animates the Ouija board. Did I say that? Yes, that's what the man said beholden to the garlands of woven fruit and beribboned cartouches, amen. What we have here are certain individuals intent on disarraying the public gravitas of things. Others, threadbare acolytes in the slow-moving sift of moulting opinion as it degrades to a screen behind which a nordic lake escapes upwards into ecstatic pastures, demur. But we began by positing the structural integrity of vapor, now it's hysteria twice over, once round the bend and two's your fancy, whatever it chooses to reveal of itself. And that is more than you get studying in a school, observing rain as it enters the rainbarrel. To think it was you that only yesterday protested the convenience of the loom's double keyboard. Now you seem launched in your own narrative, in memory's despite. The vast memorial due here fumbles its own branching hee-haw. For shame to lie like that, and over lunch. Well, it *is* due, and that's what can be said for it. I'll posit your binding resolution in the day after tomorrow's brush with de-definition. For now all bets are off.

The president always knew, under her lilacs was a liver fading. Yes, I can think of a number of things which would surprise you if you knew the soundtrack. Heterophage, we come unblinking into the standing day and tool off in several directions once our duties are accomplished. Guarding the kids, throwing junk into the adjacent yard. Sometimes the silent backup slops over the fountain's edge, and then it's a race to the unfulfilled spaces that are still blanks on the city's grid. The guardians of our tacit belonging are stilled then, we err on the sidelines and mope. The delusion comes undone with a roar. We think we have an appointment with a snowman, so is it written anyway in our datebook. But the guy just left, headed for warmer climes. And thus the breathtaking precision of our off moments drifts down the vacant plaque and its reeded copper surround. Weren't we supposed to be taking note of the new eldritch morphing into a chromatic classicism whose contour trembles like mercury, eager to be taken aboard? Alas for our foreshadowing,

for though we wander like lilies, there are none that can placate us, or not at this time. Originally we were meant as a backdrop for "civilization," the buses and taxis splurging along ring roads, anxious to please customers, though the latter proved to be in short supply. Like so many figure-ground dilemmas, this was resolved with moderately pleasing results for all concerned. Time's *arrière-pensée* floats down from on high, settles near our ankles, confirming our brush with whatever. The ensuing uproar allows us to take French leave of the other swiftly departing guests, to achieve maximum freshness once the door has closed and the great caesura of the sky, twitching with stars, fixes its noncommittal gaze on us, enabling us to stand erect and inhale huge gusts of astringent air. We are aware that we are doing something and are thus prepared to follow the event's traces as far as need be, beyond the sea and the mountains and the ridgepole at the world's end and the attendant generations.

Abruptly the season backed up. Bright green out of the red. Almost fell off my empire. On recent to-ing and fro-ing, the same old same old, the record is silent, save in vertical chirps, amounting at times to a carol, or motet. The little bomb works, it seems. Now that's one for the record books, us salivating an eternity till the sun goes down in an outer husk of our hemisphere. But a virtual contest is all it ever gets up to. A mirror shipped from halfway around the world records the whisper that begat its strangely impersonal voyage into the lap of the present, my stagger of inattention and the consequent drumroll. Invading the privacy of millions with a lurid bedtime story, the little dog laughs, climbs the stepstool bearing red carnations and lapses. The laughter begins slowly at the bottom of the orchestra pit and wells gradually toward the back; it seems to say it's OK not to be counted, you'll belong eventually even if you're not wearing the right armband or redingote. I crawled through a culvert to get here and you're right to love me, I was only a little awry, now it's my fancy to be here and with you, alright, fluted, not toxic. Prepare the traditional surprise banquet of braised goat.

You wore your cummerbund with the stars and stripes. I, kilted in lime, held a stethoscope to the head of the parting guest. Together we were a couple forever.